FIRSTMATTERPRESS
Portland, Ore.

THE
NIGHT
SKY
IS A
PLACE
WHERE
THINGS
GET
LOST

Copyright © 2019 by Andrew Chenevert
All rights reserved

Published in the United States
by First Matter Press
Portland, Oregon

Paperback ISBN 978-0-9972987-9-6

Cover Illustration Copyright © 2018
by Hellsea www.hellsea-art.com

Book design & typography
by Ash Good www.ashgood.design

FIRSTMATTERPRESS.ORG

THE NIGHT SKY IS A PLACE WHERE THINGS GET LOST

andrew chenevert

FIRSTMATTERPRESS
Portland, Ore.

AUTHOR'S NOTE

In what began as an excuse to justify reading a lot of comic books, the poems collected in this book all begin with lines from comics/graphic novels selected in a semi-random way. Apparently most of the successful poems came from assorted Bat Family books or things written by Brian K. Vaughn. The poems in this book have no other relation to their comic book sources except for a spiritual sense of zaniness and maybe some lovingly convoluted plot elements. For interested parties and/or the legal department of the Walt Disney Company, the first lines and their sources are outlined in the following table of contents.

CONTENTS

VOL 1

3   "I want to have a private conversation"
    Hale, Joshua Fialkov. *The Bunker, Vol. 3*. Oni Press. 2015.

4   "Then what the fuck is it?"
    Vaughn, Brian K. *Y: The Last Man Vol. 6: Girl on Girl*. Vertigo. 2005.

5   "But when your mother wiped symbols away"
    Carey, Mike. *The Unwritten Vol. 2: Inside Man*. Vertigo. 2010.

6   "Shut it down. No more campaign."
    Humphries, Sam. *Citizen Jack Vol. 1*. Image Comics. 2015.

8   "my books show pictures of evil"
    Johnson, Daniel Warren. *Extremity Vol. 2: Warrior*. Image Comics. 2018.

9   "This is what I will be wearing at the moment of my greatest triumph:"
    Slott, Dan. *The Amazing Spider-Man: Flying Blind*. Marvel Comics. 2012.

10 "I saw the footage of you at the National Mall"
    Vaughn, Sarah and Luna, Jonathan. *Alex + Ada Vol. 3*. Image Comics. 2015.

11 "Can you take these cuffs off? I have to go to the bathroom"
    de Campi, Alex. *No Mercy Vol. 2*. Image Comics. 2016.

12 "Okay, put your hand up, make a fist."
    Simone, Gail. *Batgirl, Vol. 3: Death of the Family*. DC Comics. 2014.

13 "You think something called 'Angel Dust' would be a happier drug"
    Remender, Rick. *Deadly Class Vol. 4: Die For Me*. Image Comics. 2016.

14 "I was growing bored with human conversation"
Millar, Mark. *Superman: Red Son*. DC Comics. 2003.

15 "I told you to call me death-bird"
Lobdell, Scott; Waid, Mark; Nicieza, Fabian; Loeb, Jeph. *X-Men: Age of Apocalypse Omnibus*. Marvel Comics. 2012.

16 "The open mic of the damned"
Seeley, Tim. *Revival Vol. 5: Gathering of Waters*. Imagine Comics. 2015.

17 "How much is a superhero birth worth to you"
Bendis, Brian Michael. *Jessica Jones—The Pulse: The Complete Collection*. Marvel Comics. 2014.

VOL 2

21 "I smell sequel"
Bendis, Brian Michael. *Ultimate Spider-Man: Ultimate Collection Vol. 2*. Marvel Comics. 2009.

23 "Get cured of being a monster."
Tynion, James, IV. *Batman: Detective Comics Vol. 2: The Victim Syndicate*. DC Comics. 2016.

25 "You gave me the wrong brain, didn't you?"
Chaykin, Howard; Moench, Doug; Barr, Mike W.; Maggin, Eliot S. Elseworlds: *Batman Vol. 1*. DC Comics. 2016.

26 "Maybe I was a happy kid"
O'Malley, Bryan Lee. *Scott Pilgrim Vol. 2: Scott Pilgrim Vs. The World*. Oni Press. 2005.

27 "To resurrect my son"
Tomasi, Peter. *Batman & Robin Vol. 4: Requiem for Damian*. DC Comics. 2014.

28 "Husband why must must must you always"
King, Tom. *The Vision Vol. 2: Little Better than a Beast*. Marvel Comics. 2016.

29 "Since you're so keen to follow in your father's footsteps,"
Spurrier, Simon. *X-Men Legacy Vol. 1: Prodigal*. Marvel Comics. 2013.

30 "Your mother misses your disloyal eyes"
Remender, Rick. *Deadly Class Vol. 5: Carousel*. Image Comics. 2017.

32 "my man god says"
Seeley, Tim. *Revival Vol. 6: Thy Loyal Sons & Daughters*. Image Comics. 2015.

33 "Yeah, me and Jesus just did the hand-holding thing,"
Suburbia, Liz. *Sacred Heart*. Fantagraphics Books. 2015.

34 "I doubt if this is God's duty,"
Aguirre-Sacasa, Roberto. *Stephen King's* The Stand *Vol. 1: Captain Trips*. Marvel Comics. 2010.

35 "Tell the women burned as witches"
Carey, Mike. *The Unwritten Vol. 1: Tommy Taylor and the Bogus Identity*. Vertigo. 2010.

36 "How I was their misfit, their bat in a flock of birds—"
Simone, Gail. *Batgirl Vol. 5: Deadline*. DC Comics. 2015.

37 "You know what they say about pictures:"
Vaughn, Brian K. *Y: The Last Man Vol. 7: Paper Dolls*. Vertigo. 2006.

38 "It looked like a rainbow—a living rainbow,"
Soule, Charles. *Letter 44 Vol. 1: Escape Velocity*. Oni Press. 2014.

39 "Your eventual parting of ways will be as sudden"
Vaugh, Brian K. *Saga Vol. 7*. Image Comics. 2017.

40 "You've been hacking your way through these trashy romance novels"
Vaugh, Brian K. *Saga Vol. 8*. Image Comics. 2017.

41 "There are questions of your guilt and culpability"
Tynion, James, IV. *Batman: Detective Comics Vol. 4: Deus Ex Machina*. DC Comics. 2017.

VOL 3

47   "I was sent here to tell you that god is very disappointed,"
Vaughn, Brian K. *Ex Machina, The Deluxe Edition Book Five*. WildStorm. 2011.

48   "Welcome to the adult team."
Walden, Tillie. *Spinning*. First Second. 2017.

50   "Do you plan on eating this year,"
Bendis, Brian Michael. *Ultimate Spider-Man Vol.1: Power and Responsibility*. Marvel Comics. 2001.

52   "I've gone atomic for you,"
Castellucci, Cecil. *Shade: The Changing Girl Vol. 2: Little Runaway*. DC Comics. 2018.

53   "It's not a forcefield"
Priest, Christopher. *Deathstroke Vol. 1: The Professional*. DC Comics. 2017.

54   "Bin Laden working at a 7Eleven"
Diggle, Andy and Johnston, Antony. *Daredevil: Shadowland*. Marvel Comics. 2011.

55   "Maybe we are in the right place after all"
Wilson, G. Willow. *Ms. Marvel Vol. 2: Generation Why*. Marvel Comics. 2015.

56   "We're alone here on the moon"
North, Ryan. *The Unbeatable Squirrel Vol. 1: Squirrel Power*. Marvel Comics. 2015.

57   "We can tame it with the coat"
Castellucci, Cecil. *Shade: The Changing Girl Vol. 1: Earth Girl Made Easy*. DC Comics. 2017.

58   "I believe we met on the roof the other day,"
Bendis, Brian Michael. *Daredevil: End of Days*. Marvel Comics. 2012.

60   "Because for a moment we share our deaths"
King, Tom. *Batman Vol. 2: I Am Suicide*. DC Comics. 2017.

61   "I sit and think about charms and talismans,"
   Busiek, Kurt. *Astro City Vol. 1: Life in the Big City*. WildStorm. 1999.

62   "I have a lot of silver at home"
   Shaw, Dash. *Cosplayers*. Fantagraphics Books. 2014.

63   "He needs sleep to heal and dope to sleep"
   Aaron, Jason and Latour, Jason. *Southern Bastards Vol. 3: Homecoming*. Image Comics. 2016.

64   "It's more imagination than memory,"
   Rucka, Greg. *The Old Guard Book One: Opening Fire*. Image Comics. 2017.

65   "The son of heaven deplores"
   Carey, Mike. *The Unwritten Vol. 6: Tommy Taylor and the War of Worlds*. Vertigo. 2012.

66   "He called up to the sky, 'why.'"
   Seeley, Tim. *Revival Vol. 4: Escape to Wisconsin*. Image Comics. 2014.

67   "You're an expert on what everyone loves aren't you?"
   Aaron, Jason and Latour, Jason. *Southern Bastards Vol. 4: Gut Check*. Image Comics. 2018.

68   "Never thought I'd sympathize with the teachers in John Hughes movies"
   Slott, Dan. *The Amazing Spider-Man Vol. 3: The Fantastic Spider-Man*. Marvel Comics. 2012.

69   "Flat water is a peasant's broth"
   Wertz, Julia. *Tenement, Towers & Trash: An Unconventional Illustrated History of New York City*. Black Dog & Leventhal. 2017.

70   "To live a life only have it end in oblivion:"
   Seeley, Tim. *Revival Vol. 8: Stay Just A Little Bit Longer*. Image Comics. 2017.

71   "This is a car. This is a lamppost."
   Waid, Mark. *Daredevil Vol. 2*. Marvel Comics. 2012.

I want to have a private conversation
no mosquitos   buzzing in my ears
no stars exploding   in your galaxies

how do you relish   quiet times
before the bang   of a glass shattering

have you ever looked   beyond the page
to the next one   elegantly blank
the urge to fill it   with charcoal expanse

befuddled   by vague constellations
when I ask   how did you get here

in response   you will let
the planets do   their drifting
while a distant earth   wages war

and another stretches   to a thin band
into the mouth   of a black hole

Then what the fuck it is?
If it's not made of cheese,
if it's not a set hastily assembled
in the confines of a Sherman Oaks studio
with pierced holes in black fabric
to imitate oblivion,
what the fuck *is* the moon?

I've thrown enough stones into the sea
to know rocks don't float
no matter what you do for them.
And now you want to tell me this one
jettisoned itself off our planet
to hang over us, playing marionet

with the tides. One false move
and we're all submerged
like every stone I've ever known.

But when your mother wiped symbols away
and images were pulled apart from their meaning,
you tried to gnaw the bark off trees,
tried to paint each blade of grass.
Everything you made you made again.
The reflection in the mirror

turned to letters, some angles whose relation
left a question. Who named the doorjamb?
How did red come to mean stop
and also passion? You had time to linger
in the metaphysical, I hope,

finally started to see the world behind each word's
dim aspects.

Shut it down. No more campaign.
No more posturing on TV
while sweat-beads loom
behind the makeup.

No more kissing babies
while lying to their parents
about how I would never,
ever, eat a baby, then later
in the bathroom licking
my lips for just a taste
of newborn flesh.

Nor more canvassing
the neighborhoods of those
who etch my face in a pentagram
on dry gray factory walls.
No more hiding my horns
beneath a hideous toupee.

No more telling the paper
the bumps they noticed
were just stress acne.
No more shouting *Fire!*
when the public finds my record
of sucking marrow from the bones
of the lower class. No more dreaming

up wars out of boredom.
No more closing the windows
to drown out the screams
of irradiated peasants.
No more writing in the list
of my least favorite skin-tones.
No more cheap gas poured
on our burning city.

my books show pictures of evil
the warm faces of dictators before they turned
the smiling demagogue in the *kiss the cook* apron
serial killers holding hands with their wives
swaths of purple tones that bring eternal night

the bitter years leading to divorce
sometimes they show photos
of people on the street
who seem in a rush, sometimes babies

sometimes we're left with numbers
configured in random order
mysterious symphonies
the tan streaks of the mona lisa

gps coordinates, things that live
in trenches in the sea
sometimes you, sometimes me

This is what I will be wearing at the moment
    of my greatest triumph:
a fresh coat of skin to make me feel like someone I've never been,
a smile, hopefully not but most likely jorts,
ten long years of accumulated grime,
hairs that don't stop growing,
the memory of you,
a billowy coat, cool-guy-shades,
blueprints of tattoos,
gallons of sunscreen,
enamel pins, sawdust wax,
one sandal, one sneaker, the flip without the flop,
a t-shirt that reads *call me when you get this*
in thick white letters

all to cover up the brain's ecstatic gymnastics,
the organs plunging inward,
the bones that yearn to liquify
under the waning moon,
which is what I've decided the night will be wearing,
that and a shawl of stars, the impenetrable black
of morning's late arrival.

I saw the footage of you at the National Mall
where you laid down in front of the monument
and pretended it was your dick before, hours later,
becoming president. Remember when you thought

The National Mall was just the Mall of America?
How disappointed you were to find no American Apparel
in the Capitol Building, to learn the pool wasn't full
of Orange Julius, just cherry-flavored Kool Aid

used as a metaphor like the trees that erupted the day
your train derailed and somehow only you survived.
I've heard you've taken shelter in a forest
plucked from a fantasy novel, which you've painted white

like your old house. You miss the sounds of ghosts
whispering presidential secrets, miss the carpet's plush,
the way everyone called you *mister*. At least you can still
lie supine in front of a fir tree and pretend

someone's taking a picture. The roots will bore
through your hips, deep into fertile soil.

Can you take these cuffs off? I have to go to the bathroom

with my full range of mobility lest I warp your new wood floors
spurting free, a garden hose unattended,
a snake with its tail cut off. I've been in clean places before

with walls so white you can see the eyelids of your shadow,
but never so tethered to myself, unable to sink
into the privacy everyone deserves. Actually
I've never even been cuffed before, especially not in a place

where full novels are monogrammed on each towel.
Nothing stains. I'm convinced that if I pissed myself
I would either die instantly or it would evaporate.
A tiny cleaning crew would burst from my urethra, mops in hand.
Can you give me back my hands?

I promise you can bind my feet and I won't crawl away.
I need to crack my knuckles, pick my nose, put my hands in my pants
to get a little warmth in this cold place.

Okay, put your hand up, make a fist.
Release and repeat. Disentangle those blood vessels in your brain.
Squeeze them out like beet juice, like the stew that comes
from hours reading the comments section.

Crush the web of thoughts in your palm.
Snort the dust because why not. Snort all types of dust.
See what happens. Dress up like a cat. Burden the neighbors.
Stalk the night with a baseball bat.

Fly banana cream pies into the face
of the aristocracy. Crumble the suburbs. Slurp them up
from a Dixie cup with a gurgle. It's like
a corn chip's rough edges rappelling down your throat.

It's like fingers staining pages. It's like a plunging market value,
mafiosos sunburning in lawn chairs by a vat of oil.

You think something called "Angel Dust"
    would be a happier drug
something like all your good times ground together
and delivered on the whole notes of heaven's choir
or strung between the strings of a harp   light as a cloud
like the rays of sun you used to think were God

deep into your trip you figure
it probably took a lot of dead angels to come to the name
and they might not have known their bones were to be powdered
so it starts to make sense   you gnashing your teeth
till they too begin to take on dust qualities
and then something in the other room tells you
to turn that racket down   but you don't remember
playing tennis or ever putting music on

least of all the type with strings swollen to bursting
least of all the kind that lifts your body upward
toward the disapproving finger wag of a god
who looks a lot like your father   or was it your mother
who is slapping you in the face and whispering wake up

next morning when the blinds worm their way open
and the silver dawn inches through them you swear
you see ten cherubs dancing on the beam   rub your eyes

I was growing bored with human conversation
and aspiring toward animal. Crouched down at the sidewalk,
I asked the ants what it's like to carry ten times their own weight.
Do they ever feel like maybe they're what keeps the earth
from hurtling into the sun? Just tiny bodies congealed into a field
to repel space's void?
                      They replied, *no.*

And so off I went, past the begging cat,
the songbirds whose Sinatra standards grew stale,
and onto the horse, who had never thought of humans
riding on her back to be an act of dominion,
and with her eyes newly opened kicked down the fence and fled.

I was looking for a ride back home, mine having departed,
when the mouse scattered out of the woods
and into a clearing, blaring
                                this is not what I wanted
as the hawk tipped down and took it in his talons,
pushing his body in a graceful movement
back into the air, guiding us insubstantially toward something:

the moment when the trees open their eyes and stones grind their teeth
against the dulled edge of all our endeavors,
and I'll run out of things to say to everything.

I told you to call me death-bird
not love-bird, not shit-bird anymore.
I'm no longer the doves exploding
from the white sleeve of a magician
at your wedding. I'm the raven
stripping off bits of carrion
from the rabbit behind the altar.

I know you don't believe me, but seriously.
Listen—my melodious trills
speak of nothing but violence
and fire in the tufts of trees. I see
pigeons outside an expensive restaurant
and the economy collapses.

Those dirt-stained rats
should live in the soupy underground
rising up to consume at my command
if that makes sense.

The open mic of the damned
where every poet's voice is stretched into a wail
and every guitar string snaps into the eye
of the loneliest audience member
who sips a drink of nails, maraschino, and lye

where every vocal melody devolves into Bon Jovi
and each piece of performance art ends in defecation
where the mic only produces a ringing
that brings every eardrum to immolation

whose idea was it to have this in a dive bar
rather than in the back alleys of hell
surrounded by buildings adorned with spikes
and the you know tintinnabulation of the bells

how can my set of Replacements covers go over
when the bartender peels her skin off
it's too late to turn back here we go I'll quaver
until per usual a fiery circle opens in the floor

and out pops the club owner demanding
one drink minimum for his no cover.

How much is a superhero birth worth to you
if they were to broadcast it on pay-per-view?
Would you gather with masses in a dive
to put your bet on the pool of potential powers,
the familiarity of dried beer sealing
the memory of cleanliness within?

This year the odds are good on X-Ray vision
and vicarious personality disorder,
but the curmudgeon beside you remembers
the good old days of super strength,
flight, invisible women. Don't throw a punch
when he asks if you think they're naked.

Tomorrow the baby takes the gamblers by surprise,
bursting out of the womb with a head that's all teeth,
eyes echoing from its stomach,
the telepathic impetus to kill.
Only Stan the barman collects any funds,
but you insist that telekinesis should count
for partial credit as your house disappears
and reappears miles out of town.

I smell sequel
or is it languid rot
the cracked egg
of rebirth
some primordial scream
catching-on to white noise language
in the static your ghost
exhales in monochrome

I am hardwired
to quote Die Hard
at your funeral

like you would have wanted
Happy trails, Hans
polite chuckles
when we approach
body's penumbra

there is an outpouring of rain
in the place I remember you best
I wish I could say
you were carried on a fleet
of black umbrellas

into the nourishment of earth
instead you are a yolk
throbbing dully
while inside something rebegins

Get cured of being a monster.
Find your fangs receding back into the gum.
Trim the claws off warty hands.
Scrub villagers' blood from nights ago
off the corners of your mouth.
Learn to French kiss again.
Go to a spin class.
Take a hike to breathe in
the baffling scent of evergreens.
Don't chase the other hikers.
Say a prayer for each victim.
Gather them as stones in a circle
and draw a line between each one.
Apply for a job. Get a credit card.
Learn how to use a toilet.
Forget the taste of flesh.
Bask in solitude.
Gather the splinters of your old life
and weave them into a new routine.
Adopt a pet. Adopt a second pet
after eating the first in a lapse.
Call your mother. Tell her
you're coming home.
Wade out into the sea

when it's hard to be strong.
Dissolve into green foam.
Carry tourists to shore
after they swim out too deep.

You gave me the wrong brain, didn't you?
I asked for the kind that can tolerate
long car rides with a full bladder.
I wanted the type where each new wrinkle never smooths,
where sometimes the moment of being is all it needs.

Once on my back under stars, I felt mine
vibrate until pink turned black and blue.
I can only imagine the latest model: my desire, humming
with ease in the background of the body,
remarking the perfection of a summer breeze, or marveling

at falling leaves, yada yada. This brain's sometimes gently pleased,
at least, by things that push away from their bearings:
a summer blockbuster with feeling, a simile slightly akimbo,
the way the fizz of soda crisps to silence on the tongue.
It just seems to fear the quiet, damp moments before sleep

when, as if from all that blackness, something will rise,
take it in its knowing claws, and suck out the juice.

Maybe I was a happy kid
all sandbox playing and stung
by arcane mastery of the sticksword
possibly a bit too ambitious though

maybe I was a happy kid
who saw dictators living in the breeze
swaying bony trees in late October
while dressed as my own ghost

I think I was a happy kid
who got everything he wanted
like most happy kids do
so there can be no doubt when I say

maybe I was a happy kid
no doubt like there must be
to question what comes next maybe
the forest is burning and we just watch the wind

To resurrect my son
I wrapped Band-Aids around his voodoo doll,
tried concentrating very hard,
read his diaries and thought of all the places
he mentioned going, all of them missing

his silhouette. The playground swing moves
with no one and no breeze.
The water fountain splashes for no one.
In scratches imitating his script,
I wrote the final entry:

March 3: Today I was hit by a car.
It was very bad. All in all I guess
things just have a way of ending.

When I looked up, there he was,
standing in the doorway, broken body
back together. Some ashen aura in the eyes,
ushered in by a halo of flies.

Husband why must must must you always
        split atoms in your gaze gauze
when peering down into the muck must
        of an unsettled trash bin. Toss the bag
bag inside where it will where will it

        remain to rot for days of rot until
it can be scooped by being bye
        the routine things we've come to
rely up and down upon. Garbage
        or trash (noun) disposal is the only
non-malfunctioning part left in our
        hourless society. Turbulent greenery

growing from the bin where we've been bin
        overwriting old programs. Learning basic
algorithms to dispossess our possessions.
        Every item in once in a
dampened dumpster slicked with sick rain—

        the sky's gray refuse refusing—is stripped
of its function. No one left on which
        for it to lean, no homes to brighten

the bright warm bright parts. Sky wet with with-
                ering clouds. Body's electric spark.

*Since you're so keen to follow in your
      father's footsteps,*
start getting to bed early, start carrying some unnamed weight
like a character in a mid-century novel. Let it fill every room
with a thick musk, invisible, untouched. Let the joie-de-vivre
leak from crow's feet when you hear someone make a joke.
Learn how to fake a smile. Never get angry enough.

Wake before the sun rises, long after your last rooster gave up,
after the foxes ate the hens. Savor the damp chill
of dawn, after the moon goes to sleep.
When driving, maintain a steady speed.

At Dairy Queen, try not to make a pass at the Chill Staff.
Laugh too hard at everything she says. Later in the bathroom
feel a touch of shame. Drive back home.

At night, sit hours while the TV imitates intimacy.
Let a log splutter to ash on the fire while you stay up to hear
news anchors offer glimpses of future.
Know life is only going

in the moments you're in your head.

Your mother misses your disloyal eyes
now that you've returned home from years away
with something resembling a need to stick around.
She's shocked when you set the table,
each neatly arranged fork, a conduit.
She's waiting to see if you'll need a ride
to the Greyhound station. Or worse another five
to pay some scheming landlord.
But in the coming days, when nothing seems to shift,
and you learn how to steam clothes with an iron,
press out all the wrinkles, and yes, even fold,

she knows someone's missing. No more pipe bombs
stuffed into the neighbors' mailbox, no more filling
the fishbowl with Jell-O instead of water.
It's been years since she last found you crusted at the curb
after curled branches left marks in your skin.
Now, only soft recognition:

something invisible glazed over your face,
a longing to stay and sit in the room illuminated
by sitcom glow, to eat a dinner while talking
about rising insurance premiums and how to be
a good and productive person, and how
to become content when days flow cleanly away

until, finally, you doze off and she watches your once tiny body,
swearing she sees the spirit leave with every breath.

my man god says
pay attention to me
let me know if you want
to chill this sunday
as the week leaks its last
rays into the next

bring the bud light
i'll bring an eternal fire
the scent of lavender
and innumerable hummingbirds
play your cards right
and i'll stop time for a bit
watch all the evils of the world

take a pause before the deathblow
the lovers caught in an endless sigh
we've got *family ties* to catch up on
we've got popcorn to materialize
an endless supply of red vines
don't ask me what it's like in the clouds
i'll tell you it's quiet
so cold so distant

Yeah, me and Jesus just did the hand-holding thing,
not the tongue thing, not the blood-meets-body thing,
instead we kept it G-rated on our tour of heaven.
I marveled at the rose gardens, the picket fences.

Imagine your home in a suburb of heaven.
On top of the fridge is a sin jar, stacked high
with one-dollar bills from each time you thought

the word *tit-fucking*, every time you slept till noon.
How engorged would yours be?
How could you hide the riches from your childbearing wife,
your dogs, your cable news networks,

from Him and his damp palms? When we reached
the outer limits of heaven, where the wicked live
in their studio apartments, with boils on their necks,
that dull anonymous pain, Jesus let go of my hand.

Here is where you will sleep. He pointed to a grave
as if I wasn't already there. As if I didn't know
the sound of fireworks muffled through the dirt.

I doubt if this is God's duty,
to keep eyes on traffic violations,
to spin the *Wheel of Fortune* for the poorest mother,
to relegate dust bunnies to the least used corner,
to watch that a loose shoelace doesn't slide underfoot,
or to make sure my bones don't turn to powder
after slipping off a ledge. He seems more concerned

these days with hurricanes, earthquakes,
the summoning of great waves,
ideologues, monologues, and snake tongues.
When the world is always so close to ending, how can he
find time for the personal crises that chip paint off our psyches?
Are feelings made cold so he can use their chill
to stop New Orleans from drowning years later?
Does the force of someone's stubbed toe
knock a rock into place to plug a dam?

In the silence, I've found some self to tend to.

Tell the women burned as witches
the last lights they see are not the flames of hell
but the white of a page removing its words,
that the corners of this world are blackened and curled
by things we're afraid of losing, that I'm sorry.

Tell them now nothing's changed,
just the manner of execution. We deliver
fire remotely or find
other ways to cut out the tongue.

No spells cast to shield you from apology,
no houses left on which to place a pox,
just waters writhing with the weight of ancestors,
watch us jump in claiming warlock in a town

that's ground its murders into industry,
that's plastered your melting faces on pub windows,
or worse, a world that does everything
to make the circle break, to interrupt the incantation.

How I was their misfit, their bat in a flock of birds—
fur where there should have been feathers,
the thirst for blood when I should have sought worms—
I'll never understand. Some duckling before the egg
had its chance to float down the wrong part
of the river, I came gushing from a womb,
fangs bared, days from flight.

In a gnarled nest, my first memory: regurgitation.
I still can't soar in perfect V formation,
always lagging behind like a statement
of defiant punctuation. In my blindness, I see
our wings are all that bind us.

One day a gust of air will carry me
back into the cave where I came from,
away from birds pushing off into the sun.

You know what they say about pictures:
their subjects move every time you look away,
so soon your grandmother will be off frame,
somewhere beyond the border of her paper world.

She had a real life once, living in your town,
which often felt like a postcard: snow
on rolling fields, the sharp reds of autumn. In spring
she kept a garden, spent years on her knees loosening
each tendril's grip on the soil

before herself melting into soil.
She's grateful she escaped
her thousand word limit.

A lot of life is lived in the photo album,
she said, before streaking dirt between pages.

It looked like a rainbow—a living rainbow,
though it was probably just a puddle of oil and sun glow
left on the asphalt where you had been
yesterday, or the day before,

where you drove off in late afternoon
with groceries: two gallons of milk for the boys,
a box of cereal for your daughter, a paperback
for the unending quiet of night.
Maybe this glow is the shadowy impression

of the moment you blipped out of time—
the unlikely meeting of red through violet
your final joke, your abstract painting left to last
after your body. Or was your gas tank just punctured?

The aesthetic coincidence of your final mark
is cordoned off and overcasts the melon stand.
Are you hanging behind the clouds,

shining pale light down on the sea and forest
but forgotten under the parking lot's hot halogen?

Your eventual parting of ways will be as sudden
as an early morning clap of thunder
and the shrieking of trees,
creaky reeds turned afloat in rain;

as prolonged as a mountain split by ice,
miners rappelling down the fissure to harvest gems;
as impersonal as a bank teller's *how was your day*

and your *pretty good*; as tender as the sun
shaving down its light by degrees,
until it's replaced by the thin silver band

of the moon's late waning; as silent
as a cat's footfalls when she's hunting;
as breathless as a fish; as distorted as the voice

reaching out from TV static
when the house is dark and no one's up;
as sentimental as dew on an iris.

When the time comes, by tomb or too much,
let each second ring. Take it in. Exhale.

You've been hacking your way through these
            trashy romance novels
like you're trying to recover a lost civilization
where legend says someone once wanted to touch you.
You are pressing the pulp into testaments
and burning palm leaves to send smoke signals.
You've gotten used to rain-soaked nights, the prowl of jungle cats
outside your tent, the whine of mosquitos,
but never the cold that haunts the empty bed.
You swear one night you saw blue eyes
blinking in a thicket—you know you are close.

You go on like this until coming to a clearing,
or maybe you find a twig unnaturally bent, a footprint,
a spearhead, blood, etc. You follow the trail
until you come across a small hut buried in the mouth of a cave
with walls lined by the same dime store books
that used to keep your warm.

You take your time in the approach,
gather the evidence to make sure this is the right way to walk,
to determine if you're good enough to enter,
until you know there's no way not to,

so I guess you do.

There are questions of your guilt and culpability
in the movie adaptation of my lassitude,
which took 27 years to climax,
bored all you theater patrons,
killed some of you probably,
and burned a hole through the screen.
The story swirls with a score
composed of infantile whining,
the off-key quavers
of love notes locked in the mind.
In the audience voting round
I can hardly blame you for favoring failure;
a revolt against a story with no conflict.
Anything to spice up the hours
you'll spend watching my hours
watching a screen turn blue until
my eyes become too bored to feign openness.
The actors play their parts
as if they've never been in any other picture.
Doesn't it seem like with each chapter
the screen gets a little smaller
where other faces cut off at the border
until there's just a close-up of my eyes
darting back and forth? That's art.
That's what art is, at least I think.
I'm hoping for the sequel but

most things end before they're ready.
Go get a popcorn and wait
years on years for a tearful reunion
with a beloved pet,
eight-hour single-take shots of me sleeping,
the brief high of a sex scene.
If you can last the whole maybe 80 years
and you've grown old in the theater,
fed on nothing but diet Coke, candy,
the slightly burnt buttered popcorn,
I hope you'll think it's worth sticking around
after the credits for a Q+A with, let's say god
where all of us may finally learn exactly why.

I was sent here to tell you that god is very disappointed,
but I can't sell it with a straight face,
that sharp-gravel-on-bare-feet variant of hell.

Instead I can tell you he's off somewhere else,
maybe getting lost with his friend in the woods,
or spending a weekend at a sports game
he won't remember when the beer clears,
inhabiting the spaces between your words

and mine. Maybe he's skipping stones on a lake,
bored waiting for his parents to pick him up
but they never show. Maybe he's pressing his flesh
against someone else's flesh and saying he'll
make her see him, which gets confusing,
so instead he settles on *I love you.*

Maybe god lives in the full moon
that I know for a fact you looked at tonight

probably while I was looking at it
and remarking how I wished I was looking at it
with you.

Welcome to the adult team.
Where once you built cities out of blocks,
we'll now be engaging in constant drafting,
painstaking bricklaying,
competitive taxpaying,
and of course nights of ever-present dread.
You caught your last cartoon
some sunny Saturday,
a bowl of cereal sweating in the summer,
too much sugar and the thought it can't get better.
Well, maybe you were right, maybe not.
Tomorrow we'll be running drills
on filling out job applications,
late night talks about what it all means,
team-based lovemaking,
learning to lose gracefully,
timeless suppression,
where to leave a semi-colon.
Our uniform consists of ties
slipped around the neck,
pantsuits to leak through,
the highwire antics of disrobing for the bathroom.
The field: an array of cubicles
broadcasting vague nothings

to a far-off alien too tired to invade.
Cheerleaders pyramid while shouting
To speak my truth . . .
I feel that . . .
Did you get the memo . . .
Best practices . . .

Do you plan on eating this year,
on folding the calendar's pages over themselves,
dipping the landscapes,
                puppies,
                              firemen, etc. in oil,
letting the ink seep with each day
until the entire thing resembles memory—
its blurred, undefined mess—
more than the potential the months once held.

The time now lives inside you
in what you justify
as embodying permanence,
                a new year's resolution.

You marked off the days you were supposed to fall in love,
scrawled V-A-C-A-T-I-O-N across weeks,
set aside the time for a friend's wedding,
an unexpected funeral,
        predicted when it would rain.
Someone once asked you why
you crossed out each day as it ended
when you weren't counting down to anything.

You replied,
*everything eventually
counts to something.*

Can you remember what you waited for
in the hours before midnight, frying up
the year, biting into everything
you thought could have been
though also everything that was?

I've gone atomic for you,
not subatomic, not bomb atomic,
the swift division, the blinding light,
more like I am reduced to my beginning,

so I can somehow be part
of the structure of you. Your cells,
the molecules of breath,

spliced universes inside
wondering how to slide through
my tinny walls,

the vibrating core,
the hum of a generator
maintaining a city block
so silent the insects can't hear it.

It's not a forcefield

that thing that keeps you
from dipping your fingers in
a puddle of your dreams,

it's a flash of will,
the gases swirling
in a neon question mark.

It's not a tank
that keeps lobbing shells
on the beach where I want to take you,
it's just the moon,

that twisted mirror ball
conducting the ocean's disco.
A home without a body.

It's not a trigger
that coaxes its gun along,
it's the silence of night,
the click of a keyboard

writing its own memoir.

Bin Laden working at a 7Eleven
Hitler flipping burgers at McDonald's

Mussolini fumbling with the price-checker at Dollar Tree
        Kim-Jong growing fat watching daytime TV

Trump unclogging your toilet

in the next life
a cockroach gains sentience

the flea that stated the plague
                does time in Alcatraz
the people who hurt you
become saplings in an already crowded forest

and you are the gold dust
        that streams down from the sky

I am the vapor released from a skywriter's plane
spelling out
      is this thing on?

Maybe we are in the right place after all
and this planet's insignificance is just a smokescreen.

You spark supernovas when you snap your bubblegum,
suck out oxygen with a kiss.

Last week I put my head to the pillow
and didn't know I was slapping together a haphazard god.

Or maybe everything we've done just hangs there—
the time you tripped at school,
the way you build a tolerance to hardness—

till the solar system's
a mound of fossils in a riverbed.

No gray can fill space,
or the body,
its parts pumping
softly in the dark.

We're alone here on the moon
but for the space between us
louder than any person
further than the distance back
to the roaming earth
its wars its hideous phases
its crystal waters receding
what book are you reading
in the hole I dug for us
I want to tell you
about the knowledge knocked
from my head the first time I saw you
I want to write a story
in our undisturbed footprints
I want to be wrapped up
in the static flag
we're alone here on the moon
as we are at the beach
as we are at our cubicles
as we are when we sleep
but somehow more so
in the flicker of dust
our dwindling oxygen
surrounded by all these stars

We can tame it with the coat
the hat the scarf
until winter walks blind
judas goated all the way
off the pasture
and spring comes in
and all that it entails
the sounds of your neighbors
screwing loudly
through windows with dust cracked loose
the shallow suspicion
of anyone with a stumble
but most of all
the way everything seems to open
and life is reduced
through greatly expanded
to fizzy drinks on a patio
stopping to say
this will be perfect
while never speaking
in anything but future tense
as we are remade
in the image of our beginning

I believe we met on the roof the other day,
in the city's balcony,
just you and I and construction material:
some screws, a molding board, a hammer.

I wanted to watch the tiny players underneath
crawl through day-to-days with eyes
just slightly glazed. You wanted rain
to touch invisible parts of your skin.

So we didn't talk, just thought
of how long it would take
to build a home up here
with our limited supplies.

        I banged each block of wood into place
        until it resembled stability
        and from some hearth roared a fire
        and from some ward sprung our child,
        the death rattle of dual rocking chairs
        not far behind, the holding of a hand,
        the slipping out of our bodies . . .

Then a siren cracked from below
And the whole thing disentangled.
The logs of our new life tumbled
to the street where they were spirited away
by men in orange vests.

Because for a moment we share our deaths
as we decided to share our lives, I stop to wonder
who cleans the litter box when the other is gone,
who levels the uneven photo frame?
With whom are the dishwashing days alternated
now that there's a void?

Who will keep the other
from seeking their own grave
when barometric pressure dips?
Who will grab the hand
of the one too quickly
crossing traffic? You'll swear
it's just the breeze on your fingertips.

Surely there's a disconnect
or the feeling of constantly leaning
to the left when walking alone.
Look how the cat marks the doorjambs
with its scent, slowly overwriting
what lingered before.

Let's not think of this tonight,
burrowed in our bed, haloed by light pollution
and rocked to dreams by our breathing.

I sit and think about charms and talismans,
tchotchkes and knick-knacks, things to ward off
unfamiliarity, or the feeling you get
when you enter an empty apartment—the last noonlight
reverberating on waxed hardwood.

I sit and think, when the time comes, and when
the big moon's erased itself into bare
resistance, about summer nights and winter mornings,
the smell of woodsmoke, the sound of rain,

the warm glow inside and the stars outside.
I sit and think by my television, where I let it
do the thinking for me, about characters
and how to make a human out of words.
How so many cities have been inhabited
only by words, and how so many still will be.

I have a lot of silver at home
now that I've got sympathy for inanimate objects.
Who knows when I'll need to melt it down
to kill a werewolf or make a neat bracelet
for your wedding night? Who am I to deny its life?

Yesterday, I saw your old shoe in the trash,
covered by the red sauce of two-nights old dinner,
and became inconsolable. Cake scraps bunching up
where once your toes rested.
It will die buried in earth like everything.

Now, I'm filling my house with what I can save:
newspapers from your birthday, the dead
cat's toys, ships long since freed from their bottles,
even the shards of glass that could have carried love letters.

If all the things we keep could sing,
I think a minor chord would swell from everything.

He needs sleep to heal and dope to sleep
and a sense of back alleys to get dope,

and to know the back alleys, he needs a rough upbringing,
parents who left him alone for days with one frozen pizza,

and for a rough upbringing, he needs some preexisting pain
that wrapped itself around the ancestral heart

back when they were single-celled,
growing with them in a fever pitch, a malignance,

and for that malignance, silence had to explode
or god had to sneeze once, spinning the cosmos

into the molten wreck it is today.
And for god to sneeze, some kid had to put pepper

in the pistil of a handsome, pink flower;
for silence, some infantryman had to throw a grenade

into the pitch black void that begins and ends in sleep.

It's more imagination than memory,
the idea of feeling your way out of a dark cave
head first into the tumult of birth,
the room a frozen lake,
the rush of senses trampling each other

and you, held under the lamp, examined
like they want to find your watermark,
thinking you'll remember this moment
for the rest of your life. How can you
forget the all-at-once of it?

You're just beginning to grasp
something unspoken under the surface:
the mouth turning upward meaning yes,
the water in the eyes, in this case, meaning yes.
You're piecing together the rules for being,

imagining you won't forget them
when the hospital lights are gone
and you're already homesick on the ride home.

The son of heaven deplores
the confusion of a single rose
hanging on a limp stem
the interpretations of the moon

words without meaning
and the impossible act of being
poised against himself
by a cloud-covered sky

the beauty of a mountain
the daily goodbyes
when things slip invisibly
the sun enacts the clock

its only lines the ones it left
sitting against your skin
years ago one summer
in the dense heat of newness
fresh defiance in your blood

all the times we thought time
would circle around in the end
wrap us in its blanket
or tie us in its rope

He called up into the sky, why.
    To which the sky only replied
        with a half-smile, the moon's dim sliver,
            and a little twinkle in its eye.

As if it was saying *be patient, it'll come,*
    what you're waiting for. A trace of sun
        buried itself across his face
            the taste of salt flecked on his tongue.

When something burns in the asking
    keep your questions trapped
        in the place behind the tooth
            until they slip through the cracks

into the night sky where things get lost
    to float through stars like wandering ghosts.

You're an expert on what everyone loves aren't you?
Whether it's the shift into autumn air,
nostalgic candy dispensers, traveling an unlit desert road,
it's written in your encyclopedia.

You know the way my knees break at the sound of trains,
the way a laugh flushes my chest with helium,
my tears at a flock of birds or the cold coffee you left me
six hours before I woke up, turning in the daylight.

But what is it that you love? You'll never tell
the songs that send you back home, what to say
to soften the edges of your night, the star you first
thought might guide you, how to dream.

Never thought I'd sympathize with the teachers in John Hughes movies

but here I am poised to break against my own lack of discipline,
wishing I could pass down the detention sentence,
my dried lips quivering, all the youth drained from my eyes,

wishing I could be the ruler to the knuckles of love
instead of someone trying to fit together the clues as to why
you never showed up to class, why the world seems a little less bright

without your bass-bass-snare manners, your movie montage beauty.
I could be the no-nonsense mustache, my only purpose to be ruffled
by a birthday cake collapsing under candles, boys collapsing under
       blushes.

But,

I would rather be the New York you get lost in
when you think you're alone. And yes, I know,
John Hughes didn't direct that one, but it's better than staying home.

Flat water is a peasant's broth.
Raise me rich on white rapids,
salt-swollen oceans,

the two day-old beers
we abandoned on the counter
before we fell asleep.

Make me a meal of sand
and the bands of oil
following a freighter ship,

braise it in the sun turning
water to a rainbow,
or fill me with the thirst

quenched like every time we wake up
and you've brought a glass

of water, flat, from the sink
but I still end up a king.

To live a life only to have it end in oblivion:
Is there a greater relief than knowledge
your debts will vanish with one blow,
your suitcase can stay unpacked,
the room you spent your days rearranging will be filled
with someone else's things? Does the body

plan its obsolescence so the you of you
can fit into a shiny new model, capable of processing
the things you never could: sad loves, war,
the desert in a superbloom.
The new you who has time for second thoughts
deserves a long life

where past traumas only show up in dreams,
like relatives returning from holiday
with slideshows you endure.

When they leave, and you latch the door,
the sunlight fills the room and you feel as though
you've dropped your luggage off
in some far place bristling with palm trees,
the trickle of water calling you home.

This is a car. This is a lamppost.
This is daylight. This is nightshade.
This is a record spinning in reverse.
This is the human heart's slow pulse.

Will you learn to differentiate
between a kick drum and your love,
though both keep you invisibly moving,
like trying to trap air inside a room?

This is a broken window. This is your childhood
obsession with highways. This is a field
of wildflowers crossing the brain's wires.

Can you try to ascertain
which neurons you set off
when you lit the house on fire,
which spark slammed shut the door?

This is a mosquito floating in your yard.
This is a sun disappearing in the ridge line.
These are the last days of our lives
or maybe they are the first.

ACKNOWLEDGEMENTS

Warm thanks to everyone from the Eastside Poetry Workshop who looked at these poems and many others week after week. It feels great to have found a community and friendships with such dedicated and conscientious writers.

Credit where credit is due to the comic creators, whose lines I've shamelessly ripped off, and the artists who bring their words to life. Thanks for the hours of entertainment and inspiration.

My gratitude to Lauren Paredes, Ash Good, and Kassandra Lighthouse with First Matter Press for encouraging this book and giving these eccentric little poems a home.

Lastly, thanks to you for being such a dedicated reader that you're even looking at the acknowledgements. Pat yourself on the back. Take a walk. Feed your dog.

ANDREW CHENEVERT
lives in Portland, OR, where he is the co-founder of the Eastside Poetry Workshop. His work has appeared in several journals, including *Clarion*, *Side B Magazine*, and *Anesthesiology: The Journal of the American Society of Anesthesiologists*, which is pretty weird but very cool. This is his first book.

www.ingramcontent.com/pod-product-compliance
Lightning Source LLC
Chambersburg PA
CBHW070438010526
44118CB00014B/2091